<u>WHALES</u>

BELUGA WHALES

<u>JOHN F. PREVOST</u>

ABDO & Daughters

Published by Abdo & Daughters, 4940 Viking Drive, Suite 622, Edina, Minnesota 55435.

Library bound edition distributed by Rockbottom Books, Pentagon Tower, P.O. Box 36036, Minneapolis, Minnesota 55435.

Printed in the United States.

Cover Photo credit: Peter Arnold, Inc.

Interior Photo credits: Peter Arnold, Inc.

Edited by Bob Italia

Library of Congress Cataloging-in-Publication Data

Prevost, John F.
   Beluga whales / John F. Prevost.
     p. cm. — (Whales)
Includes bibliographical references (p. 23) and index.
   ISBN 1-56239-477-0
1. White whale—Juvenile literature. [1. White whale. 2. Whales.] I. Title.
II. Series Prevost, John F. Whales.
QL737.C433P74 1995
599.5'3—dc20   95-6374
                                         CIP
                                         AC

ABOUT THE AUTHOR
John Prevost is a marine biologist and diver who has been active in conservation and education issues for the past 18 years. Currently he is living inland and remains actively involved in freshwater and marine husbandry, conservation and education projects.

Contents

BELUGA WHALES AND FAMILY

Beluga whales are **mammals** that live in the **Arctic Ocean**. Like humans, they breathe air, are **warm-blooded**, and feed their young with milk. They are one of the most **vocal** whales.

Another name for the beluga is the sea canary. Their loud chirps and whistles are heard through boat **hulls** and **aquarium** walls. They are also called white whales. They are the only truly white, meat-eating whale.

The beluga's only relative is the **narwhal**. Both whales have adapted to life in the **arctic**.

Beluga whales are also known as white whales.

SIZE, SHAPE AND COLOR

Beluga whales are 10 to 16.5 feet (3 to 5 meters) long. Males are slightly larger than females. A thick layer of **blubber** keeps them warm. The thick body makes their head seem small.

Beluga whales have a large melon-shaped forehead. Like all whales, belugas breathe air through a **blowhole**. It is located slightly to the left of the forehead's center. Their **flippers** are short and wide.

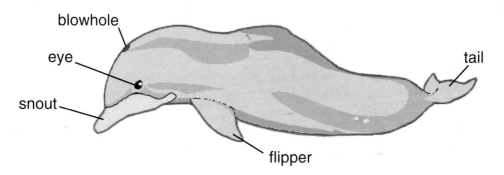

Toothed whales share the same features.

Beluga whales have a melon-shaped forehead.

Instead of a **dorsal** fin, beluga have a row of bumps on their back. Beluga whales are born gray. They turn white as they get older.

WHERE THEY LIVE

Beluga whales live in **arctic** and **sub-arctic** waters. They move south when temperatures drop and the **ice pack** thickens. Small **pods** of up to 12 whales will join into **herds** of hundreds. A small group of family members makes up each pod.

During the spring and summer, beluga whales may move into fresh water to find food. Some belugas stay in waters which do not ice over and have plenty of food.

Detail Area

Beluga whales are migratory animals that move south in the winter months.

SENSES

Beluga whales and people have 4 of the same senses. They have good eyesight in and out of the water. Belugas are curious creatures. They will bob their head to see above the water surface.

Because they are **social** animals, touch is an important sense. Touching allows them to show feelings and **communicate**. Belugas have a sense of taste. They can tell when they enter salt or fresh water. Beluga whales do not have the sense of smell.

HOW ECHOLOCATION WORKS

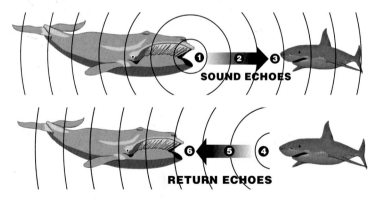

SOUND ECHOES

RETURN ECHOES

The whale sends out sound echoes (1). These echoes travel in all directions through the water (2). The sound echoes reach an object in the whale's path (3), then bounce off it (4). The return echoes travel through the water (5) and reach the whale (6). These echoes let the whale know where the object is, how large it is, and how fast it is moving.

This beluga whale is bobbing its head to see above the water surface.

Hearing is the beluga whale's most important sense. Because of its thickness, water passes on sound better than air. Belugas use sound to find **prey**. By making loud clicks and whistles, these whales will listen to the returning echoes to "see" around them. This is called **echolocation**.

DEFENSE

Killer whales, polar bears, and man hunt beluga whales. Killer whales find them in open water, and chase the young or weak in a **pod**. Using their senses to see danger, beluga whales can avoid killer whales.

Polar bears will hunt belugas they find in shallow water. Beached belugas will lie still and will look like a mound of snow or ice to the bear.

Humans have heavily hunted beluga whales in some areas. Now, hunting laws protect them.

Stranded beluga whales will lie very still so that polar bears won't see them.

FOOD

Beluga whales hunt for food in fresh and salt water. They eat worms, **mollusks, squid,** shellfish and fish.

Belugas squirt water into the sandy or muddy bottom to find hidden **prey**. Fish are caught in the beluga's slightly curved teeth.

Beluga whales hunt in groups to trap **schools** of fish and squid. They use **echolocation** to find prey in dark and cloudy water. Beluga whales will also follow large groups of fish and squid.

Beluga whales hunt in groups.

BABIES

A baby beluga whale is called a **calf**. At birth, it is about 5 feet (1.5 meters) long. A beluga calf is gray or brown with many small dark spots. As it grows older, the spots will fade. When it becomes an adult in 5 to 9 years, a beluga calf will turn white.

Beluga calves need their mother for food and safety. Calves will **nurse** for at least 20 months.

A beluga whale mother and her calf.

BELUGA WHALE FACTS

Scientific Name: *Delphinapterus leucas*

Average Size: 10 to 16.5 feet (3 to 5 meters)

Where They're Found: All around the world in **arctic** and **sub-arctic** waters. Will travel into fresh water.

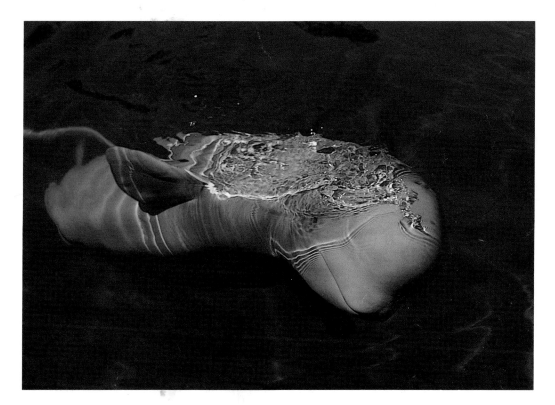

The beluga whale.

GLOSSARY

AQUARIUM (uh-KWAIR-ee-um) - A building used for showing collections of living fish, water animals, and water plants.

ARCTIC (AR-tik) - At or near the North Pole.

ARCTIC OCEAN - The ocean of the north polar region.

BLOWHOLE - A nostril (or nostrils) found on the top of the whale's head through which it breathes air.

BLUBBER - A thick, fatty layer found under the skin of many sea mammals.

CALF - A baby whale.

COMMUNICATE (kuh-MUH-nih-kate) - To exchange feelings, thoughts, or information.

DORSAL (DOOR-sull) - Of, on, or near the back.

ECOLOCATION (ek-oh-low-KAY-shun) - The use of sound waves to find objects.

FLIPPERS - The forelimbs of a marine mammal.

HERD - A group of animals of the same kind.

HULL - The body or frame of a ship.

ICE PACK - A large layer of floating ice formed by pieces of ice that are pressed together and frozen into a single mass.

MAMMAL - A class of animals, including humans, that have hair and feed their young milk.

MOLLUSK - An animal with a soft body, often protected with a shell.

NARWHAL (NAR-wall) - A small-toothed whale found in the arctic seas. The male has a long, twisted tusk.

NURSE - To feed a young animal or child milk from the mother's breasts.

POD - A herd or school of whales or seals.

PREY - Animals that are eaten by other animals.

SCHOOL - A group of the same animals traveling and living together.

SOCIAL (SOE-shull) - Living in organized communities.

SQUID - A sea animal having a soft, round, tubelike body, a pair of fins, and ten arms.

SUB-ARCTIC - The areas near the arctic circle.

VOCAL - Having to do with the voice.

WARM-BLOODED - An animal whose body temperature remains the same and warmer than the outside air or water temperature.

Index

BIBLIOGRAPHY

Cousteau, Jacques-Yves. *The Whale, Mighty Monarch of the Sea.* N.Y.: Doubleday, 1972.

Dozier, Thomas A. *Whales and Other Sea Mammals.* Time-Life Films, 1977.

Leatherwood, Stephen. *The Sierra Club Handbook of Whales and Dolphins*. San Francisco California: Sierra Club Books, 1983.

Minasian, Stanley M. *The World's Whales*. Washington, D.C.: Smithsonian Books, 1984.

Ridgway, Sam H., ed. *Mammals of the Sea.* Springfield, Illinois: Charles C. Thomas Publisher, 1972.